Additional praise for the Tiny Book of Thoughts series

"Tiny thoughts - - tiny but profound is all I can say! Very, very inspiring!"
- **Lauren MacLauclan**, author of *The Law of Attraction 'How–to' Book*

"Thank you so much for your wonderful books – your quotes are marvelous and our readers will love them...Your Thoughts and energy are deeply appreciated."
- **Lee Simonson**, Publisher of *Heartwarmers* and *Petwarmers*

"Small books with big wisdom."
- **Peace Pilgrim II** – renown peace advocate and author of *Enjoying the Journey*.

"A wonderful collection of introspective and inspiring thoughts that can change your life."
- **L. Fownes**

TINY THOUGHTS FOR PERSONAL TRANSFORMATION

Also by Karl Schmidt

A Tiny Book of Thoughts
ISBN: 0-9686831-0-x

A Tiny Book of Thoughts Too
ISBN: 0-9686831-1-8

Another Tiny Book of Thoughts
ISBN: 0-9686831-2-6

The *Tiny Books* each contain just over 70 aphorisms/thoughts, many of which are found in this book, and the books themselves are physically small (3"x5"). The tiny books were self-published and were not widely distributed and I only have a few copies of each left. If you are interested in purchasing these please contact me via the email addresses on either of the following websites:

www.TinyThoughtGuy.com

www.WorldofWonder.ca

Aphorisms/thoughts not included in this book, as well as additional ones, will be shared in a future book.

Electronic versions of this book include:
PDF - ISBN: 978-0-9686831-4-9
MOBI – ISBN: 978-0-9686831-5-6
EPUB – ISBN: 978-0-9686831-6-3

TINY THOUGHTS FOR PERSONAL TRANSFORMATION

change your thoughts, change your life

Karl Schmidt

Inspired Crow
Publications

The necessary legal stuff

Published in Canada by Inspired Crow Publications

Cover design and photography by Karl Schmidt

Library and Archives Canada Cataloguing in Publication

 Schmidt, Karl, 1968-, author
        Tiny thoughts for personal transformation : change your thoughts, change your life / Karl Schmidt. -- 1st edition.

 ISBN 978-0-9686831-3-2 (pbk.)

        1. Aphorisms and apothegms. I. Title.

PN6271.S353 2013   158.1   C2013-904333-0

Dedication
- In Gratitude -

I am a firm believer that in order to grow, just like everything else in nature, we need three things: a foundation, energy/light, and nutrients.

My Foundation

These are the people that were there from the very beginning and, although some of them have since transitioned to the next part of their journey, I am forever grateful to them for giving me the foundation, the initial tools that were so crucial for the start of my journey. Without the tools and care given to me by these people I would not have had the foundation to build upon and after floating around aimlessly I would have likely wandered off course. For their gifts and guidance I give heartfelt thanks to: Mom, Dad, Oma, Karl, the Universal Force and Gaia.

My Light Bringers

These are the individuals with whom I have shared a portion of my journey and who have positively enriched me with their essence and presence. Although my intention is to express my gratitude to each and every person that fits into this category, there probably are not enough pages in this book, so I will focus on acknowledging those who have had, in my biased opinion, the most profound impact. For those not appearing on this list, please know that I still appreciate all you have done for me and you are forever part of my experience. You have my eternal gratitude and I wish all of you unbounded happiness.

Elisabeth K., Amy D., Don E., Leah E., Mark O., Al S., Dave S., Duane P., Eric B., Gard P., Jeanne P., Mike D., Gerry V., Ian M., Geoff S., Melanie D., Ron B., Don D., Mehdi S., Peace P., Heather P., Nils H., Renate H., John A., Joy B., Gerry V., Dean E., Larry M., Grant J., Corey S., Nicole W., Ian M., Martina T., Bette-Anne W., Adele W., Nancy T., Paula M., Marilyn G., Cheryl A., Ian M., Sheridan V., Lara H., Nel L., Simon L., Karin L., Tom M., Carol Irene W., Pete O., Wilma F., Diane J., Brock T., Shiva V., Darrell R., Darren R., Dennis J., Janice H-W., Joan W., Rita B., and the crows.

My Nutritionists

This section could also have been titled, "My Manure Bringers", or even, "My ….(oh, I guess I'm not allowed to use that phrase=;0). As with the previous section, there are a vast number of people that I could include here, but you didn't honestly expect me to give you a list did you? In all seriousness though, there are a great number of people with whom I have interacted where the experience might not be labeled as "pleasant." This does not mean however that the experience was any less valuable than those experiences that I would label as joyous or pleasant. It is my firm belief that there are two main types of experiences in life: those we enjoy, and those that force us to grow. In many ways, the experiences that we consider unpleasant or that are associated with our greatest obstacles are often the precise experiences we need to propel us forward. To all of the people on this list I express my gratitude for helping me to learn some of the most important lessons on my journey thus far and for tolerating my lack of awareness.

Namaste.

"All that we are is a result of what we have thought."
Buddha

Acknowledgment
Thank you to the "Do Crew"

I call the folks listed in this section the "Do Crew" because even though they did not directly collaborate on this project, their actions and support have allowed me to "Do" this project. I extend my gratitude to the following people: Dave, Brad and the rest of the team at *Photo Experts* for helping me process my photographs – including the one on the cover; Wayne Longstaffe for keeping all the essential parts moving; William at Crystal for keeping my technology ticking; Karina for renting me the cars that helped me journey to so many inspirational places; Shaun, Tabitha and the folks at *KKP* for taking care of my printing needs; Tom, Michael and the folks at *Banyen* for all of the work they do to bring awareness to my world; Mo for all of her dedication in looking after the crows, and finally, for allowing me to feel the music that energizes me, I want to thank Peter Gabriel, Alanis Morissette, Pearl Jam, Jesus Jones, Collective Soul, Angels and Airwaves, Yes, Foo Fighters, Hennie Becker, David Arkenstone, Jay Scott Berry and Bruce BecVar.

WARNING

Just like the waistband on a cheap pair of underwear that does not go back to its original form after it has been stretched by one too many desserts, so too is the mind unable to contract after being exposed to new ideas. If you decide to read this book, or even if you just open it up and read a single thought, your mind will be altered forever. Perhaps by reading this book your life will be enriched, perhaps not. Perhaps you will agree with some of the information on the following pages, or perhaps some of the information will irritate you. Perhaps the meaning behind some of the aphorisms will be blatantly clear and obvious to you, or perhaps you will find some of them vague and confusing. With this book **I only make one guarantee and that is: after reading any, some, or all of the information contained herein, your life will never be the same**. Just by the mere fact that you have read this, your life is impacted. I believe that, "***Experience is a process, not an event***" so ANYTHING and EVERYTHING that we come into conscious contact with will forever alter our consciousness and therefore, it is extremely important that we selectively choose what content we allow into our minds. With this book my intention is to share some thoughts/aphorisms that will add to your journey in a positive manner: I believe they will. At this point I should also mention how I define an "aphorism." I see an aphorism as a brief or short saying that embodies a general truth or observation. Certainly some debate can be had as to what is merely a thought and what is an aphorism; I don't want to enter into that debate here. My desire is to share some ideas, concepts, thoughts or aphorisms, whatever label you choose to use, that have been part of my journey and my truth. I will share more in a moment about how I see "My Truth" in relation to "The Truth."

Well, that's it. That's the warning message. If you have made it this far, you might as well read the actual introduction.

**Please note that this text and the images in this book are deliberately large in size to assist those with visual impairments.

INTRODUCTION

Good morning. Perhaps by the time I finish writing this it will no longer be the morning, and perhaps for those of you reading this, it's already later in the day; however, I need to start where I am.

First and foremost, "Thank you" for taking the time to read the introduction: it is a key component to understanding what it is that I am trying to do with all of this ink on paper (or if you are reading this on an electronic device, with all of these zeros and ones). I must admit, my own tendency in the past was to usually skip the introduction of a book and get right into the main content. Certainly there are times when this works just fine, but there are other times when the introduction is actually a key component that prepares the reader for the content. In a way I guess it is similar to fast forwarding a movie to the "good parts" and not "wasting time" with the "other stuff." Although one can still enjoy a movie by watching it this way, a great deal is lost in the process.

With a book like this, and by "this" I mean a book with small bites of information and no explanation, I believe that it is important to understand the essence of

what I'm doing in order for you to get the full benefit of the material. Because, (weren't we always told in school never to start a sentence with the word "because?") **the aphorisms and thoughts contained on these pages are very concentrated**, I consider this book to be the "advanced course." As such, the reader is left to ponder these aphorisms on their own and I do not provide any personal opinions as to what I believe they mean. I did not include any analysis or opinion, not to frustrate the reader or to be aloof; rather, I believe that it is important for the reader to expand their awareness through the process of contemplation, rather than by simply reading a concept and then having me give my "biased" opinion. This is to say that while there is "The Truth" the only thing that we are actually capable of sharing is "Our Truth", a subset of "The Truth" that has been influenced by our experiences and perceptions. We are unique in an infinite number of ways and, as a result, our truth cannot be somebody else's truth. Our uniqueness is an amazing gift that is helping us to create our reality for this journey, so for us to impose "Our Truth" is counterproductive to everyone. Furthermore, I remember some of the textbooks from school that had the answers at the back of the book. Of course, I would never just skip to the back of the book and read the answer, but I hear that some people did =;0) Okay, I confess, I did that on occasion; however, as is often the case in life, I gave the answer that somebody, in this case the teacher, wanted to hear, and then I failed the test miserably. By simply regurgitating information, by not putting in the effort ourselves, we might acquire knowledge and we might be able to impress people, yet when it truly comes to understanding something, when it comes to gaining wisdom, the truth is revealed and we are lacking.

In this book I share "My Truth" and I offer it only as a means for you to see reality from a different perspective. The aphorisms/thoughts contained on these pages were derived from meditations and moments of Satori (a Zen term for awareness or awakening). I believe that the aphorisms came through me and I was merely the scribe who recorded them. These aphorisms were pertinent to my journey at a specific time in my life, yet it seems that as life progresses they remain part of my truth. It is not my intention to give advice nor to make claims that my experiences will in any way impact your life.

To illustrate this point, when I originally put pen to paper, for those old enough to remember paper (wink, wink), a friend read over what I had been writing and said to me, "Just like that old adage, it sounds like you want to show people how to fish, rather than simply give them a fish." I mulled over that statement and, trying not to be disrespectful, went on to say that, "To me it is even more than that: my desire is simply to go fishing and to allow others to watch me fish. If there is something that I do that allows them to be better at fishing, then that is superb. On the other hand, if what I am doing does not improve what they are already doing then I do not want to impose my way of fishing on them. They should continue to do as they have been doing."

It is also important to mention that **if something in this book touches you or inspires you, that's fantastic, but realize that this book was only a spark. Any changes you make were already within you and can only be accredited to you**: **changes only come from within**. It may take time, but I truly believe that anything we do that brings more light into the world is a positive thing. Conversely, in the event that some of the information contained on these pages does not ring true for you, PLEASE leave that thought/concept behind and move on to another one.

Indeed, even in my own experience there were concepts that I initially rejected. On one occasion I remember reading an aphorism after my meditation (many times when I wrote down thoughts I would not know what I wrote until later on when I re-read them) and thinking to myself, "This is nonsense, I don't believe that at all." I crumpled up the paper and I threw the note into the garbage bin (recycling wasn't as well-known back then). Later in the day (I assume my subconscious mind had been playing with the aforementioned thought) it hit me what the thought actually meant: all of a sudden I could relate to it. I went back to the garbage, which, thankfully, wasn't full of messy, gooey stuff, and pulled out the crumpled piece of paper. For me, this is what I would term an "A-ha" moment, or, as I mentioned earlier, "Satori." So, even if an idea does not resonate with you right away, let it go, and move on. Perhaps later in the day, or even many years later, it will resonate with you. We all know that the world was flat until 1522, there were no such things as germs until the 1860's, no human will ever walk on the moon, no human will ever run a mile in less than four minutes... As I said in the warning, when we are exposed to new ideas we can't help but be challenged by them and changed by them: each of us differently.

To that end, because we all learn in our own unique way and we all resonate with different ideas, I thought it would be appropriate to retain aphorisms that might have a similar theme.

Where possible, I have added an image or graphic for those who enjoy visual cues. In some cases the graphic might relate to the aphorism/thought in a literal sense, in other cases the connection may be more subtle.

I'm hoping that some of the graphics and some of the words on the following pages will present you with your own "A-ha" moments and maybe some of the aphorisms will allow you to see your world through new eyes. My job, my journey, is simply to share the thoughts and to allow the reader to do with them as they wish; however, to get the most out of our time together I would suggest that going slowly is the best way to take this journey. Perhaps take a thought a day or a few thoughts at a time and contemplate them. With the *Tiny Book of Thoughts* trilogy, some people shared that they would like to concentrate on a situation in their life and then randomly open the pages. In some cases the thought would give them an insight into their situation, perhaps a new way of seeing a relationship or a problem. If the idea on that particular page couldn't be directly related to their specific situation then the benefit was that they could use it to take their mind off their particular issue: I call this a "Pattern interrupt." That is to say that sometimes, when we get stuck in a thought spiral, we need something to interrupt that pattern, something to "get our mind off of" a particular issue so that we can think about it from a better head-space.

When you read a thought/aphorism you might contemplate what the aphorism means to you. Do you agree with what the thought infers, or do you disagree with what it says? Can the aphorism be used to improve the quality of your thinking or the quality of your relationships? However you choose to use the aphorisms is correct, I would only suggest that racing through the material will limit its usefulness. Many ideas come to us and we simply dismiss them by saying to ourselves, "I know that already." In some cases we do understand the idea and we have incorporated it into our lives: that's fantastic. In many instances though, we say that we "know" something when in actual fact we mean that we have "heard that before" or we "get it" on a surface level, not truly understanding it. We might know that a stove can be hot, but until we burn ourselves we don't truly understand what that means. We might "know" a word in a foreign language without actually being able to use or apply it. We might "know" how to ride a bike, but if we haven't ridden one in a while we will fall off a few times. Some of us "know" that certain foods don't react well with us, but it isn't until a little while later that our body reminds us, why we should not eat that food. So, remember that there is no need or benefit to rush through this meal, it's a big course and I believe you'll enjoy it more by taking your time: savor it. Please do not be fooled by the simplicity of many of these aphorisms: they are deliberately direct and to the point, they are not meant to be lengthy and wordy. The *Tao Te Ching* is considered by many to be one of the most amazing and powerful books ever written, yet there are only 81 very short sections (paragraphs). I am not saying that the information in this book is comparable to the Tao, I am saying that we should not use verboseness as a measure of effectiveness or importance.

On another note, you might notice that several of the words have been spelled in a manner that appears incorrect; however, this spelling was intentional and these are not typos.

Finally, I wish to thank you for your patience in reading this introduction and I will leave you with this aphorism: I think it is a superb way to start your journey, ***"If you simply believe everything you read, why read?"***

That which
you keep
dies with you,
that which
you share,
lives on.

To err is human,
but to err
on the side
of compassion
is humane.

The sun
is always shining;
it's just that
sometimes
the clouds
get in the way.

If you can't find love,
maybe
you need to clean
your mirror.

Be who you want to be,
just don't impose on me.

I'll do what I want to do,
and I won't impose on you.

Accolades
and
applause
are
aphrodisiacs
for the
ego.

What our mind
does resist
there our energy
does persist.

As you believe,
so you perceive.

Evolution
is simply
perfection
in motion.

Appreciation
fosters
inspiration.

In order to grow,
we need to let go.

You're exactly
where you're
supposed to be,
because if you weren't,
you wouldn't be.

Truth
is not
a democracy.

Why listen
to the weather report
if you never
go outside?

The more we
expect,
the more difficult it is
for us to
accept.

When Death
becomes your friend,
who shall be
your enemy?

As the writer
my job
is to create:
as the reader
your job
is to debate.

Ritual
should not
take precedence
over purpose.

When you have
a heavy heart
why not let
a friend
help you hold it?

If you only do
what you know
you only know
what you knew.

You can tell
a real champion
by how hard they try
when nobody
is looking.

If you love something
hold it
with an open hand,
not a closed fist.

Even
the grandest
of mountains
will appear
insignificant
if
you move
far enough away.

Soul:
the invisible fingerprint
we leave behind
on everything
our heart touches.

The obstacles
you see before you
merely become
the paving stones
of the road
you once traveled.

Become less,
be more.

The walls
of a fortress
can easily become
the walls
of a prison.

When you
encounter
a problem
'use it',
because
'you is it'.

It's
often best not to
help someone up
until
they have
fallen down.

Beware
of too many wants
becoming needs,
otherwise
for dissatisfaction
you are sowing
the seeds.

Each day becomes a blur,
yet we still say,
'I wish I were...'

All we truly have is this day,
so let's not waste
and wish it away.

It's OK
if today isn't
the
best day of your life
because that means
there is room
for improvement.

Be the best person
you can be,
and
let the universe
take care of the rest.

The greatest part
of giving thanks
to the universe
is watching it say
"you're welcome."

If you find it difficult
to enjoy the
act of giving,
why not
start with the
act of sharing?

'Stress'
is what happens
when we try
to impose
our will
on life.

Having a need
for something
and loving
something
are two different
things.

None
of the grains of sand
beneath our feet
appear
perfectly shaped,
yet they fit together
perfectly
to create the path
on which we travel.

Couldn't
every book
be labeled
as
'self-help'?

Mightier than any sword
&
stronger than any shield
is
the truth revealed.

Just because
my love is true,
I don't blindly accept
all you do.

Once we
understand nothing
we will
understand everything.

G - *U* *IL* - T

Labels
limit.

U
R
1
so
B
1

There is
no such thing
as a
small miracle.

Does
your day
start in morning
or in
mourning?

When the head
and the heart
go to war,
the body
becomes
the battlefield.

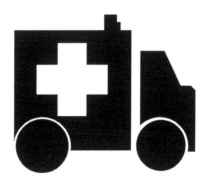

You never know...
and even if you did,
you couldn't prove it
anyway.

How can you heal
if you cannot feel?

Has there ever been
a great achievement
that did not arise
from
a great challenge?

Freedom
doesn't come from
having everything
we need:
freedom
comes from
not needing
everything
we have.

Do,
Don't do,
Up to you.

When the time is right,
on comes the light,
and you know,
the way to go.
Taste, vision, touch and smell,
in the physical serve you well,
but from the very start,
if you follow your heart,
you will hear it say,
to happiness there is no way,
for you see,
it's just…
to be.

It may
require more courage
to take the high road,
but it is consistently
the path
with the best view.

The past
is simply a compass
whose needle
points no further
than
the present.

Those who
relish the spotlight
may wish to remember
that the brighter the light
the more obvious
the shadow.

There is nothing
so loud
as a thought.

When hope
inhibits action
it simply becomes
another
four-letter word.

I don't believe
I should act
unless
my acts
support
my beliefs.

When
we fall in love
with someone,
they should grow
to be a part of
who we are,
not cause us to grow
apart from
who we are.

Of course
life isn't fair;
if it were,
why would we
be here?

As humans
we may all be different,
but the sum of our parts
makes us
all equal.

When it comes to life,
we can be
passionate
or we can
pass-on-it.

That which
surrounds you
is
within you.

If
showing
that you care
is an effort,
then you don't.

"Remember when..."
– now is
"when."

Be patient
or
be a patient.

I have yet
to find a sword
with a single
edge.

If you simply believe
everything you read,
why read?

If
you didn't have
a watch/clock,
what time
would it be?

A true holy person
wants
your arm around
their shoulder
rather than
your head
at their feet.

Fear
is
faith fallen.

When giving advice
we may wish to remember:
the more loudly we speak,
the more likely we are
to hear it echo.

Each and every day
try
to touch someone's life
in a positive way.

To the question
"why"
there truly is
no reply.

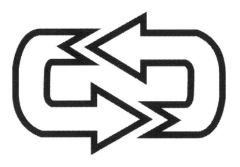

Us & we
is
you & me.

Be mindful
of activity
masquerading
as productivity.

A tongue
that speaks the truth
never tires.

Wherever
me go,
E-go.

How can one
move beyond
something
that one
refuses to see?

If your epitaph
was based solely
on what you did today,
what would yours say?

Do you want it that way?

Know
thy world
as thyself.

Determination
is not only
the ability to continue
on after defeat,
it is also
the ability to
continue on
after success.

Love
inspires,
not
requires.

The darker the night,
the brighter
the light.

Treat me as I am
and that I shall remain;
treat me as I wish to be,
and that I shall become.

Everyone
is a slave to their words,
yet it is up to us
to determine
what kind of master
one serves.

Forgive
the transgression,
but
remember the lesson.

We learn
when we are mindful,
not
when we are mind-full.

If
the longest journey
is from
the head to the heart
then
thoughts are the fog
that make it so.

Before
you take a stand,
isn't it important
to know
where your feet are?

Whether
the glass is half full
or half empty
is secondary;
it's what's inside
that counts.

The universe
has provided us
with more wonder
in our immediate vicinity
than we can hope
to comprehend
in an entire lifetime.

'Never happens',
does,
and
'always happens',
doesn't.

From
nothingness
comes
oneness.

The more
defensive we are
the more
offensive we become.

When we
make a value judgment
about somebody,
does it reflect
on who they are,
or on who we are?

Life
will never be
complete,
for those only wanting
to compete.

The more axes
we have to grind,
the more likely
we are
to cut ourselves.

Out of the corner of my eye,
I noticed the earthly days
roll by,
but when I gave them
my care...,
they were
no longer there.

It's not
always
necessary to catch,
sometimes it is better
to duck.

Sometimes
even eagles
have to walk.

*Li*f*e*
is love
with
a little 'if'
in it.

If someone you idolize
falls
from their pedestal,
remember
who it was
that put them there.

YOU
are the only one
that can
make a difference.

The universe replies
to all of our questions,
it's just that
we tend to ignore
the answers
we do not like.

Today
is a wonderful day
don't let a thief
called worry
steal it away.

Is it any coincidence
that "Love"
starts with a letter
that looks like
a boomerang?

The question
essential,
the answer,
incidental.

If I can accept
your apology
I hope
that you can too.

Fear
is the dark stranger
that can only survive
in the shadow
of the mind.

Is it you,
or is it me,
when you try to conquer,
who do you see?

Experience
is a process,
not
an event.

We do not choose
who to love
- we choose
who not to love.

H-old

O-nto

P-ositive

E-nergy

I was here,
you were not,
now you are here,
I am not.

The less we pretend,
the less we need
to defend.

The rose blossoms
in spite of
its thorns.

Is it
the optimist
or the pessimist
who carries an umbrella
in the desert?

The path
to enlightenment
is the journey
from, "why me?"
to, "yippee!"

Be
the
ripple.

Mental constipation
can often be cured
with a diet rich in
mental contemplation.

One of the surest
ways to lose something
is to
take it for granted.

Some people
spend a great part
of their lives
trying to clean
their windows
- other people
just open theirs'.

As we attach
to the high,
so too
are we imprisoned
by the low.

The more
we bypass the heart,
the greater the odds
of having
a heart bypass.

Act
until
action.

Accepting
some of the choices
we have made
might be difficult,
but for many,
a greater challenge
is to accept
the choices
that others have made.

An artist
is anyone
who extracts
beauty
from the
mundane.

Walking away
doesn't necessarily mean
giving up.

Passion
is a
necessary part
of
compassion.

There are certain
to be times when we
will have to eat
our own words
and the sweet ones
will undoubtedly
be easier to swallow
than the bitter ones.

In order
to realize your destiny,
you must be willing
to release
your history.

Sometimes
$1+1=11$

Whose
attitude
controls
your mood?

Relationships
can neither be
created nor
destroyed,
they can
only
change form.

The danger
in simplifying things
is that
we may make them
more difficult
to understand.

Are
you
hear*
to
help?

Children
are fated
to learn the lessons
that their parents
were unable
to learn.

W-ith
I -ntention
S-tuff
H-appens

How does one find
that
which was never
lost?

No matter
where
you go,
there
you are.

In keeping with
proper etiquette,
it is OK to look
at the past,
just don't stare.

The most sinister
of prisons
is the one
with
transparent walls.

True understanding
is understanding
that we don't need to
understand.

Certainly
it is our nature
to be kind,
why else
would we be
called
"humankind?"

Wings
work best
when facing
into
the
wind.

If those you meet
cannot see,
do you too
close your eyes?

Denying
the world
our natural
gifts is
blasphemy
in its
purest form.

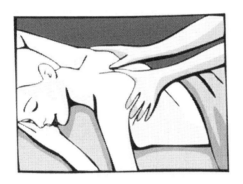

At
what
cost?

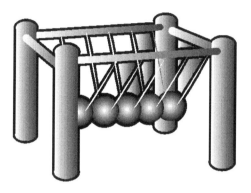

Just for the curious (officially this section is called the "afterword")

This section is only included for those who might be curious about how the original *Tiny Book of Thoughts* trilogy came to be. Well, it started in a galaxy far-far away...Nah, while that might be true, I can only speak to what has happened here, on earth, starting circa 1999, with a quick flash back to the early 1970's (and no, I'm not talking about the Timothy Leary kind of flash back, I was only about five years old at the time).

When I was a child, and I can't say exactly what age I was, only that I was around five or six years old, I would frequently have a few, different types of amazing dreams. One series of dreams would revolve around the ability to fly. While I would be soaring through various environments, both in large cities and in rural areas, in most cases these locations were not places that I had visited, in the physical sense, prior to having these dreams.

In another series of dreams I would occasionally encounter "monsters" and in the dream they would only have power over me while I stayed unaware of my own power.

When I was aware enough to know that these "baddies" could not, in actual fact not do any harm to me, I would turn the tables and send them packing. I could do this ONLY as long as I stayed aware that I had the ability to conquer them. If I fell into hopelessness or fear then it was my butt being chased.

A final series of dreams revolved around an experience that I have a hard time describing, I ended up calling it "phasing." In these dreams I was able to take small objects, and for some odd reason it was usually either a coffee cup or a small ball, and by "unfocusing" my mind I was able to turn these objects into pure energy and then "phase" them into another place. This place, for which I did not have a word for at the time, would now be referred to as another dimension: a dimension that existed at the same time and place as the current one, but in such a manner that we could not see it. I use the term "unfocusing"- which according to my spell check is not a real word- because it is the only way I can describe a process by which the intent is to free the mind of all thought. In essence, it is the opposite of focusing the mind. After having phased the object I felt totally exhausted, even in my dream state, and I would not be able to retrieve or even see the object in the other place until I had rested sufficiently to regain my energy. The largest object that I was ever able to phase was a basketball and I recall that this really drained my energy to the point of utter and complete exhaustion. Even in the dream I thought I needed a nap!

At the time of these dreams I certainly had no exposure, in the physical world, to concepts like quantum physics or even more common place concepts relating to atomic particles, molecules etc. My parents were not academics and these concepts would not have been discussed in our home, nor were they topics of discussion at school.

The common thread between all three types of my dreams was not the individual scenario so much as it was the feelings that accompanied what was happening in these dreams. It didn't matter which dream it was, they were always accompanied by these incredible feelings of, what I would now call, bliss. In addition, there always seemed to be a brilliant light, golden in color, that was associated with these feelings. The light itself was visible, more than that though, it was "felt." By "felt" I do not mean temperature wise, it was more like a knowingness, if that makes sense. Bottom line, at the time these dreams just "felt good."

In time, and again I can't say with any degree of certainty when that would have been, these dreams stopped.

Now fast forward to 1999 and these earlier, feel-good dreams of my childhood were long forgotten. The dreams I was having at this point in my life were essentially the exact opposite. I would have these horrible dreams throughout the night and awake from my sleep four or five times, only to have a new dream haunt me. These dreams did not involve ghoulish entities or "bad people" they were dreams in which I was simply an observer witnessing the heart-wrenching experiences of other people.

I recall one night in particular when I had several of these dreams. One dream involved a British bobby (policeman) who was walking his beat in the dark streets of London. As he approached one of the pubs a drunkard stumbled out onto the street and proceeded to throw up in the gutter. The policeman knelt down beside the man and tried to help him to his feet. The scene itself was certainly disturbing; however, what really impacted me was that I could feel the policeman's inner turmoil as he witnessed the scene. I felt the sorrow he felt for the person laying in the gutter in front of him. At this point I woke up and eventually fell asleep again, only to have another disturbing dream.

This dream involved a single mother coming home to a small, rundown, single room apartment. As the mother came through the door my perspective was from the upper corner of the room, looking past a single light bulb hanging from a wire in the middle of the ceiling. The room itself is very dimly lit, with dishes piled up on the counter, sparse furniture, and filled by the sounds of a crying baby. When the mother entered the room, just like the Bobby in the previous dream, I could feel her anguish. She was in complete turmoil as she analyzed her life and the life of her baby. She was suffering horribly on every level and I could feel this anguish. I was powerless to do anything other than observe. Thankfully, at this point I woke up and, although this scene ended, the "essence" of the dream replayed again and again, just with different characters. On and on it went through the night. The only commonality between these dreams was that I was a powerless observer in every one of them. There were no demons to slay or victories to be had, just people in anguish.

I realize that there are probably numerous explanations and theories as to why I was having these dreams and, in hindsight, as is often the case, I do believe I know why I had them. Regardless, that is not important in what I want to share here. The point of me discussing these dreams, and dreams of my childhood, is to add some context as to how things changed for me in 1999.

As you can see, the first part of 1999 provided me with some challenges that were giving me all sorts of grief. Thankfully, later in that same year a friend of mine performed an act of kindness, totally unrelated to my dreams or my challenges, that on some inexplicable, energetic level, shifted things for me. Literally, I went to bed as the "old me" and woke up a new person. That night the horrible dreams had vanished and had been replaced with the dreams that I had had as a child so long ago. These dreams were once again filled with flying, phasing, and vast quantities of golden light. I woke up refreshed and excited. The feelings that accompanied the long-lost dreams were once again feelings of happiness and bliss.

With the return of these new dreams and good feelings I started to seek answers as to what had happened. In the process of exploration I discovered a whole new world: a world of the unseen.

Prior to this transformation, my main belief was to "live and let live" and to be the best person I could be. In the event that somebody crossed me, then they would get back ten-fold. I never caused problems or hurt people, I just wanted to do my thing and allow everyone to do theirs'. I did not think about energies, spirituality, religion etc. If it was physical it was real and if it wasn't physical why should I care?

The morning after my transformative experience there was a significant shift in how I perceived the world. One of the first changes that I became aware of was my perception of colours (Canadian spelling, eh=;0). Prior to the transformation I had no particular interest in flowers and yet the very next day, as I was driving to work, I could not help but marvel at all the amazing, colorful flowers in the gardens of the homes en route. It was as if I had been seeing things in drab, lifeless colours and now, with this shift, everything seemed so vibrant and alive. Then, just as I was marveling at the flowers a familiar voice in my mind interjected, "Since when do you care about flowers?" It was like a mental game of Ping-Pong about why I, all-of-a-sudden, cared about these flowers. Needless to say, the old, tired view of the world was systematically being replaced with a new, curious fascination.

Again, I will fast forward past some of the other information and finally get to the point of creating the *Tiny Book of Thoughts* series. I never initially intended to write a book, not to mention a trilogy, yet, as is often the case with the universe, my plans were superseded by that of some higher power. As a very brief side note, I promise it will be brief, I did not grow up with any religious affiliation and had no knowledge of spirituality. While I have no particular aversion to using the word "God", I tend to use the terms Higher-power, Universe or All-knowing when referring to the powerful force of creation. I understand that no matter what term is used it is still be a label and therefore limited in its ability to describe the essence of what I'm referring to, yet in order to have a discussion about the concept one needs to use a label of some sort. Call the force whatever you wish, I think we are on the same page. *Now, back to our regular program.*

As I was sharing before I became sidetracked, I did not set out to write a book, my original intention was simply to record some information that "popped into my head" as I researched my transformation and the reasons behind it. My quest for answers led me to the practice of meditation and I thought that this activity might shed some light, no pun intended, on my experience. Little did I know, meditating would be the doorway down the "rabbit hole" for me.

I certainly was not, nor am I now, an expert at meditation, and often my busy mind would prattle on as I sat in the dark waiting for some answer to come to me. Over time though, in conjunction with other events in my life, I started to open up more and ideas would come to me. Originally, I did not even record the ideas. Eventually though, the same idea would come back over and over again and I found that the only way for it to leave my mind was for me to write it down. This led me to a process that I think could be called, "automatic writing." Essentially, when I was meditating I would have a pen and paper handy and when these thoughts came I would simply jot them down. Initially the thoughts were accompanied by me anal-izing (I mean analyzing) them. This usually resulted in my over-active mind interfering with the flow of information and meant the end of my meditation session.

Eventually I realized that the best process was simply to allow the information to come to me, jot it down without looking, and then later on, after the meditation was finished, read what I had written.

Some of the thoughts that I wrote down were very timely and relevant for my journey, so I decided to print out the thought, in large font, and post it at my desk at work. Some of my coworkers also enjoyed the thoughts and asked if I could print a copy for them as well. In time, one of my coworkers suggested that the ideas should be compiled into a book. I did not necessarily care for the idea because growing up I was always one of those students that dreaded doing reports: I was never able to write enough to fill the required word count. This is to say that while I did not mind writing, I always seemed to be lacking content.

Well, once again, the universe was busy making plans without my knowledge and more people suggested putting the information into a book. Finally, I relinquished and I said to the universe that if I was meant to write a book then the universe better get off its duff and send me a lot more of these thoughts. As it turns out, I learned another, unexpected, lesson: be careful when you challenge the universe or what you ask/wish for.

When I returned home from work that day, after making the challenge, my subsequent meditation was flooded with information. On several occasions I had to stop writing because my hand was fatigued.

All of this writing quickly led to having a sufficient number of aphorisms/thoughts to create a small book. The ideas kept coming though and in short order I had far more content than I had thought possible: certainly more than I could include in a small book. As I started to compile the book I read over the thoughts again and again. Some aphorisms really resonated with me, others not so much. With me wanting to limit the size of the book it was necessary to exclude some of the thoughts and I decided to exclude the ones that "I" felt were not as "important" or as "powerful" as the others. Then it came to me (and I don't want to use the idea of a voice in my head, yet that seems to be the most accurate way to describe what happened) that everybody needs to hear things in their own way and that I should not be using "my" judgment to filter what message other people will be receiving. Consequently, I used a semi—random system to determine which thoughts were to be included (little did I know that down the road I would be writing two more books wherein many of the excluded thoughts would be used).

As for the physical characteristics of the book, with the thoughts being very short and because I thought it was important for people to be able to have the information handy, I decided to make the books physically small enough to be carried in a pocket or purse. My hope was also that by making this book physically small people could easily gift it when they met somebody whom they felt could use the information. How often do we encounter somebody that might benefit from a book that is sitting at home gathering dust on the book shelf?

In addition to making the book small, I decided to include, what I perceive to be, some important symbolism: on the cover and with the content itself. I will refrain from sharing the symbolism as it applies to the interior of the book because that is something more closely related to my personal journey and likely not of much interest to you; however, I do want to speak very briefly about the cover image. This image came to me in my meditation as well, first as the triangle and what it meant and then later the yin and yang symbol.

I understand that there are many beliefs about the number three as well as with the triangle shape itself and I don't want to delve into that, I would simply like to share the message I received about how the triangle relates to my journey. The image of the triangle, at each of the three points, represents three necessary components for a successful journey in this life time: love, truth, and happiness. If any one of these three components are lacking in our life then we are in disharmony and will need to work towards adding the missing component. Please note that I do not define success here because I believe that it is unique to each individual.

In addition to the three fundamental components of a successful journey, I feel that the system in which we live needs: balance, harmony, and flow (again number three makes itself known). To symbolize these qualities, the ancient symbol known as the "yin and yang" was presented to me. Combining the two symbols we create a single symbol where the yin and yang is at the center of the triangle, touching each of the three sides.

In addition to the symbols on the cover, the color green on the cover of the first book, *A Tiny Book of Thoughts* was also a deliberate choice to represent the fourth chakra: the heart chakra. I'm definitely no expert in this field, I just went with the color that was presented to me. The colors on the covers of the subsequent two books in the trilogy, *A Tiny Book of Thoughts Too* and *Another Tiny Book of Thoughts*, are also related to the chakras.

I think that covers the creation of the *Tiny Book of Thoughts* trilogy at length and, indeed, this section actually ended up being a lot lengthier than I originally anticipated: for once in my life I actually wrote more than I thought I was going to =:0)

History = His story

As with the other section, "Just for the Curious", this section is not crucial to the book and it is only included here to satisfy the inquisitive. This section is a very brief story of who I was.

You see, just like a story in a fiction book, my history, everyone's history, isn't "real." Certainly, it was real at one brief moment in "linear" time, then everything changed and what was true in the previous moment was no longer true. As a result of this fact I can share with you who I was, but I can never say who I am because as soon as I did that it would no longer be true. I am not trying to be difficult or elusive, I just want to be accurate. So, for those seeking and wanting to answer the age old question, "Who am I?" I have great news: you can stop looking right now, grab a glass of wine and relax. In linear time you'll never be able to answer that question honestly because as soon as you do, you'll have to start all over again. Ok, Ok, fine, the answer to the previous question is that: you are all that is, all that was and all that will ever be. Now, go get that wine and meet me by the pool.

Still here? Fine, I will share a little bit more. I accept that time, as we know it, is linear and in order for a person to be 40 years old, they had to have been 30 years old and 20 years old etc. I know that if you build a bridge you start with a concept, then a plan and then add some metal and cement. If you go right to the metal and cement part it likely won't work out too well, at least I wouldn't want to drive over it. So, while we have a history - a past - and we definitely have the present and, if all goes well, a future, these are merely convenient terms and ideas that make this journey a little more orderly. However, these are just relatives and not absolutes.

In relative terms then, some of my past activities include: volunteering in a hospice, working with a positive, soul-ution (deliberate misspelling) oriented newspaper in various incarnations (it was originally called *Know News is Good News* and later on it was *The Phoenix News*), I am a founding member of, and worked on, a radio program called *News for the Soul*, I was one of the original "gurus" (I put that in italics because it was their term, and I don't care much for it) on a website called Spiritual-Tips-dot-com (a subsidiary of Life-tips-dot-com), I worked on an annual event called *Clam Chowder for the Soul,* and I have worked with various energy healing modalities (albeit not for some time now).

To me, those are some of the defining moments in his-story. I deliberately did not include the many number of jobs that I have spent time at because, while they are part of my journey, they were just a small part. More importantly, in my present, I am working on a few more book ideas, enjoying my photography, and the big one, trying to live on purpose, with intention. Perhaps I can sum things up this way:

"At the end of the day,
When I'm on my way,
I hope I can say,

I made this place,
A better space,
For the human race".

I wish you the best always, in all ways, thank you for sharing this moment.

Karl Schmidt

Cyber-homes for some amazing people

I believe that there are a great number of people who are helping to improve the quality of other people's journey and who are making their wisdom available via the Internet. This list is by no means complete and **I am in no way trying to give the impression that the people on this list are endorsing my work** (other than those explicitly quoted in the testimonials section), these are just people whose work I admire, or with whom I have had conscious contact. By "conscious contact" I mean that I have had a direct personal experience with these individuals and I whole-heartedly support the message that they are conveying. While I know that there are numerous other individuals out there doing similar work, or other inspiring work, I do not feel it is appropriate to add a connection to a person or to an organization with whom I am unfamiliar. Due to the physical nature of this book, the information on this list is current as of the print date; however, the information may be outdated by the time you read this, so I will make updates to the list on my website: ww.TinyThoughtGuy.com as frequently as possible.

Alan Cohen: www.alancohen.com

Andrew Matthews: www.andrewmatthews.com

Andrew Weil: www.drweil.com

Bernie Siegel: www.berniesiegelmd.com

Brock Tully: www.brocktully.com

Byron Katie: www.byronkatie.com

Carl Hammerschlag: www.healingdoc.com

Dan Millman: www.peacefulwarrior.com

Dan Poynter: www.parapublishing.com

David Carson: www.medicinecards.com

Deepak Chopra: www.deepakchopra.com

Eldon Taylor: www.eldontaylor.com

Gary Zukav: www.seatofthesoul.com

Gregg Braden: www.greggbraden.com

Guy Finley: www.guyfinley.org

Jack Canfield: www.jackcanfield.com

James Van Praagh: www.vanpraagh.com

Joe Dispenza: www.drjoedispenza.com

Larry Dossey: www.dosseydossey.com

Lauren MacLauclan:
www.lawofattractiontrainingroom.com

Lynne McTaggart: www.lynnemctaggart.com

Marc Allen: www.marcallen.com

Marianne Williamson: www.marianne.com

Mark Victor Hansen:
www.markvictorhansen.com

Napoleon Hill: www.naphill.org

Paulo Coelho: www.paulocoelho.com

Peter McWilliams: www.mcwilliams.com

Ram Dass: www.ramdass.org

Richard Bach: www.richardbach.com

Sanaya Roman: www.sanayaroman.com

Shakti Gawain: www.shaktigawain.com

Sonia Choquette: www.soniachoquette.com

Sounds True: www.soundstrue.com

Susan Jeffers: www.susanjeffers.com

Wayne Dyer: www.drwaynedyer.com

Zeev Kolman: www.zeevkolman.net

Manufactured by Amazon.ca
Bolton, ON